BUSINESS PLAN ALCHEMY

Transforming Ideas Into Successful Business Ventures

Peter James

Ebooksguy

CONTENTS

INTRODUCTION

Welcome to "Business Plan Alchemy: Transforming Ideas Into Successful Ventures," where the magic of entrepreneurship meets the strategic precision of business planning. In this dynamic ebook, we embark on a journey to unlock the secrets of turning visionary concepts into thriving enterprises.

Crafted for both seasoned entrepreneurs and aspiring business moguls, this guide demystifies the art of business planning, providing a roadmap to navigate the complexities of the modern market. Explore innovative approaches to idea formulation, market analysis, and financial modeling that transcend the ordinary, setting the stage for your venture's extraordinary success.

As we delve into the alchemy of business planning, you'll discover techniques to refine your vision, attract investors, and mitigate risks. From outlining compelling value propositions to creating robust operational frameworks, "Business Plan Alchemy" equips you with the tools to transform your business dreams into tangible, strategic realities.

Prepare to witness the synthesis of creativity and pragmatism, where ideas undergo a metamorphosis into well-crafted, actionable business plans. Embrace the alchemical process that leads to sustainable growth, competitive advantage, and the realization of your entrepreneurial ambitions.

Join us on this transformative journey as we illuminate the path from innovative concept to triumphant venture. "Business Plan Alchemy" is your indispensable companion on the road to entrepreneurial success, where every idea has the potential to become pure business gold. Let the alchemy begin!

Peter James

CHAPTER 1: INTRODUCTION TO BUSINESS PLANNING

Defining The Purpose And Importance Of A Business Plan

A business plan serves as the foundational roadmap for your entrepreneurial journey. Its primary purpose is to articulate the vision, goals, and strategies of your business in a comprehensive document. It is a dynamic tool that not only outlines your business concept but also details the steps required to bring that concept to fruition.

Clarity of Vision:

A well-crafted business plan helps crystallize your business vision. It forces you to articulate your mission, values, and objectives, providing clarity on the purpose and direction of your venture.

Strategic Guidance:

It serves as a strategic guide, outlining the steps you need to take to achieve your business goals. From marketing strategies to operational plans, a business plan helps you make informed decisions that align with your overall vision.

Communication Tool:

A business plan is a communication tool that conveys your ideas to stakeholders, including investors, partners, and employees. It acts as a comprehensive document that speaks to the viability and potential success of your business.

Risk Mitigation:

By conducting a thorough analysis of market conditions and potential challenges, a business plan helps identify and mitigate risks. It allows you to proactively address obstacles that may arise during the course of your business.

Financial Roadmap:

One of the critical elements of a business plan is the financial section. It provides a detailed financial roadmap, including revenue projections, budgeting, and financing needs. This not only attracts investors but also helps you manage your resources effectively.

Importance of a Business Plan:

Attracting Investors:

Investors often require a solid business plan before considering funding. A well-prepared plan demonstrates your commitment, competence, and the potential return on investment, making your business more attractive to investors.

Operational Guidance:

For internal purposes, a business plan guides day-to-day operations. It helps management and employees understand the business's objectives, ensuring everyone is working toward a common goal.

Strategic Decision-Making:

In a dynamic business environment, decisions need to be strategic and well-informed. A business plan provides the necessary insights and data to make informed choices that align with the overall business strategy.

Business Validation:

Crafting a business plan forces you to validate your business concept. It prompts you to conduct market research, analyze competition, and assess the feasibility of your ideas, ensuring that your business has a solid foundation.

Adaptability and Flexibility:

A business plan is not static. It should evolve with your business. Regularly revisiting and updating your plan allows you to adapt to changing market conditions, technology trends, and internal developments.

In essence, a business plan is more than a document; it is a dynamic tool that shapes and guides your business journey. Whether you're seeking funding, aiming for sustainable growth, or navigating challenges, a well-defined business plan is your compass in the complex world of entrepreneurship.

Outlining Key Components Of An Effective Business Plan

Outlining key components of an effective business plan involves breaking down the document into essential sections that collectively provide a comprehensive overview of your business. Here's an original explanation:

1. Executive Summary:

The executive summary is a concise snapshot of your entire business plan. It includes an overview of your business concept, mission statement, key objectives, and a summary of financial projections. Despite being the first section, it's often written last to encapsulate the entire plan effectively.

2. Business Description:

Provide a detailed description of your business, including its history, mission, vision, and values. Clearly articulate your products or services, target market, and unique selling proposition (USP). This section sets the stage for understanding the fundamentals of your business.

3. Market Analysis:

Conduct a thorough analysis of your industry, market, and competition. Define your target audience, assess market trends, and highlight your competitive advantage. A robust market analysis demonstrates your understanding of the external factors that can impact your business.

4. Organization and Management:

Outline your company's structure, ownership, and key personnel. Provide bios of key team members, emphasizing their qualifications and roles. Investors and stakeholders want to know that your business is led by a competent and experienced team.

5. Products or Services:

Detail the products or services you offer, emphasizing their features, benefits, and unique qualities. Discuss any proprietary aspects, intellectual property, or competitive advantages your offerings may have.

6. Marketing and Sales Strategy:

Present your plans for promoting and selling your products or services. Include details on your target market, pricing strategy, distribution channels, and promotional activities. This section outlines how you intend to attract and retain customers.

7. Funding Request (if applicable):

If you're seeking external funding, clearly outline your financial needs. Specify the purpose of the funding, whether for startup costs, expansion, or other initiatives. Provide a breakdown of how the funds will be utilized.

8. Financial Projections:

Offer a comprehensive view of your financial forecasts, including income statements, balance sheets, and cash flow projections. Back up your projections with realistic assumptions and data, demonstrating a thorough understanding of your business's financial landscape.

9. Risk Analysis:

Identify potential risks and challenges your business may face and outline strategies for mitigation. This section shows foresight and preparedness, enhancing the credibility of your business plan.

10. Appendices:

Include any supplementary materials, such as detailed financial statements, market research data, or additional documentation that supports and strengthens your business plan.

An effective business plan weaves these components together, creating a cohesive narrative that instills confidence in potential investors, partners, and stakeholders. Each section serves a unique purpose, contributing to a holistic understanding of your business and its potential for success.

Setting The Stage For Strategic Thinking And Long-Term Success

Setting the stage for strategic thinking and long-term success in your business plan involves creating a foundation that aligns with your vision and goals. Here's a guide in original language:

1. Visionary Introduction:

Begin your business plan with a visionary introduction that clearly articulates your long-term goals and overarching vision for the business. Convey a sense of purpose and inspire confidence in the potential success of your venture.

2. Mission Statement:

Develop a concise mission statement that encapsulates the fundamental purpose of your business. This statement should reflect the core values and principles that guide your strategic decisions, setting the tone for strategic thinking.

3. SWOT Analysis:

Conduct a comprehensive SWOT analysis (Strengths, Weaknesses, Opportunities, Threats) to evaluate internal and external factors influencing your business. This strategic assessment helps identify areas for improvement, potential advantages, and key considerations for long-term planning.

4. Clearly Defined Objectives:

Outline specific and measurable objectives that provide a roadmap for your business's growth. These objectives should be aligned with your long-term vision and serve as milestones to gauge progress over time.

5. Market Trends and Forecasting:

Demonstrate strategic thinking by thoroughly analyzing market trends and forecasting future developments. Understanding the dynamics of your industry allows you to position your business for long-term success by proactively adapting to changing market conditions.

6. Competitive Positioning:

Clearly define your competitive positioning within the market. Identify your unique selling proposition (USP) and competitive advantages that will contribute to your sustained success. Articulate how your strategic approach sets you apart from competitors.

7. Long-Term Financial Planning:

Develop a detailed financial plan that extends beyond immediate goals. Include long-term projections, cash flow forecasts, and investment plans. This financial roadmap aligns with your strategic vision and provides a clear path for achieving sustained success.

8. Innovation and Adaptability:

Emphasize your commitment to innovation and adaptability. Communicate how your business is poised to evolve with emerging trends and technological advancements, ensuring long-term relevance and success in a dynamic business landscape.

9. Risk Management Strategy:

Acknowledge potential risks and challenges and articulate a robust risk management strategy. Demonstrate foresight and preparedness by outlining contingency plans, ensuring that your business can navigate uncertainties and setbacks with resilience.

10. Continuous Improvement and Feedback Loop:

Highlight your commitment to continuous improvement. Establish mechanisms for gathering feedback and adapting your strategies based on market responses, customer insights, and changing industry dynamics. This iterative process is crucial for long-term success.

By integrating these elements into your business plan, you not only set the stage for strategic thinking but also establish a foundation for sustained success. Your strategic approach, coupled with a visionary outlook, positions your business for longevity and adaptability in a competitive marketplace.

* * *

CHAPTER 2: EXECUTIVE SUMMARY

Crafting A Compelling Executive Summary As The Gateway To Your Business Plan

Crafting a compelling executive summary is essential, as it serves as the gateway to your business plan, capturing the attention of readers and providing a snapshot of the entire document. Here's a guide in original language:

1. Concise Business Overview:

Begin with a concise overview of your business, summarizing its nature, industry, and key offerings. Clearly articulate what your business does and its unique value proposition in the market.

2. Vision and Mission:

Express your business's vision and mission succinctly. Share the overarching goals and purpose that drive your company. This sets the tone for the strategic direction outlined in the rest of the business plan.

3. Key Objectives:

Highlight the primary objectives of your business. Whether it's achieving a certain market share, expanding into new territories, or introducing innovative products, outline the specific goals that will guide your business's growth.

4. Market Opportunity:

Clearly define the market opportunity your business aims to capitalize on. Discuss the demand for your products or services, market trends, and any gaps or opportunities that your business is uniquely positioned to address.

5. Unique Selling Proposition (USP):

Articulate your Unique Selling Proposition (USP) – what sets your business apart from competitors. Clearly convey the distinct features, benefits, or advantages that make your offerings compelling in the market.

6. Target Audience:

Define your target audience or customer base. Identify the demographic, psychographic, or geographic characteristics of your ideal customers. This demonstrates an understanding of your market and potential customer needs.

7. Business Model:

Briefly explain your business model, including revenue streams, pricing strategies, and sales channels. Provide a high-level overview of how your business generates income and sustains profitability.

8. Achievements and Milestones:

Showcase any notable achievements or milestones your business has accomplished. This could include successful product launches, partnerships, or significant growth. Highlighting past successes instills confidence in your ability to achieve future goals.

9. Financial Snapshot:

Offer a snapshot of your financial status. Include key financial metrics, such as revenue figures, profitability, and any significant financial achievements.

This provides a quick glimpse into your business's financial health.

10. Funding Requirements (if applicable):

If seeking funding, clearly state your funding requirements and the purpose for which the funds will be used. Specify the amount you're seeking and how it aligns with your business objectives.

11. Call to Action:

Conclude the executive summary with a compelling call to action. Encourage readers to delve into the complete business plan for a more in-depth understanding of your business's potential and strategic direction.

By weaving these elements into your executive summary, you create a compelling narrative that entices readers to explore the details within the full business plan. Keep the language clear, engaging, and focused, ensuring that the executive summary serves as an impactful gateway to the comprehensive insights that follow.

Summarizing The Key Elements Of Your Business, Mission, And Goals

Summarizing the key elements of your business, mission, and goals in a business plan requires clear and concise language that encapsulates the essence of your venture. Here's a guide in original language:

1. Business Overview:

Begin by providing a brief overview of your business. Clearly state what your business does, its industry, and the products or services it offers. Avoid unnecessary jargon and focus on conveying the core identity of your business.

2. Mission Statement:

Summarize your mission statement in a sentence or two. Highlight the fundamental purpose and values that drive your business. This statement should articulate the underlying reason for your business's existence and its commitment to certain principles.

3. Vision for Success:

Share your vision for success succinctly. Describe the future state you aim to achieve with your business. Whether it's becoming an industry leader, pioneering innovation, or reaching a specific market share, convey your aspirational goals.

4. Unique Selling Proposition (USP):

Clearly articulate your Unique Selling Proposition (USP). Summarize what makes your products or services unique and compelling in the market. This could include features, benefits, or qualities that distinguish your business from competitors.

5. Target Audience:

Provide a concise description of your target audience. Outline the demographic or psychographic characteristics of your ideal customers. This demonstrates a focused understanding of the market you aim to serve.

6. Key Objectives:

Summarize the key objectives your business aims to achieve. These could include short-term and long-term goals related to market penetration, revenue growth, customer acquisition, or other strategic milestones.

7. Business Model:

Briefly explain your business model. Summarize how your business generates revenue, including pricing strategies, sales channels, and any unique aspects of your financial approach.

8. Market Opportunity:

Highlight the market opportunity your business is positioned to capitalize on. Summarize the demand for your products or services, market trends, and any gaps or opportunities you aim to leverage.

9. Commitment to Sustainability and Ethics (if applicable):

If sustainability and ethical practices are integral to your business, briefly mention your commitment to these principles. This can be a succinct statement conveying your dedication to responsible business practices.

10. Call to Action:

Conclude the summary with a call to action, encouraging readers to explore the detailed business plan for a comprehensive understanding of your business's mission, goals, and strategic direction.

Keep your language clear, avoiding unnecessary complexity, and ensuring that each element is summarized effectively. This approach will provide readers with a quick yet comprehensive overview of the key aspects of your business without resorting to plagiarized content.

Hooking Investors And Stakeholders With A Concise Overview

Hooking investors and stakeholders with a concise overview in your business plan involves crafting a compelling narrative that quickly captures their interest. Here's a guide in original language:

1. Captivating Opening:

Begin with a captivating opening that sparks interest. This could be a thought-provoking statement, a relevant industry statistic, or a compelling question that sets the tone for the rest of the overview.

2. Elevator Pitch:

Craft a concise elevator pitch that summarizes your business in a few sentences. Clearly communicate what your business does, its unique value proposition, and the market opportunity it addresses. This pitch should be impactful and easy to remember.

3. Unique Selling Proposition (USP):

Highlight your Unique Selling Proposition (USP) early on. Clearly articulate what sets your business apart from competitors. This could include innovative features, superior quality, or a niche market focus that gives your business a competitive edge.

4. Market Opportunity:

Provide a brief overview of the market opportunity your business is tapping into. Summarize key market trends, the demand for your products or services, and any gaps or underserved areas that your business is positioned to address.

5. Traction and Achievements:

Showcase any existing traction or notable achievements your business has attained. This could include successful product launches, strategic partnerships, or significant customer acquisition milestones. Demonstrating early success instills confidence.

6. Scalability and Growth Potential:

Emphasize the scalability and growth potential of your business. Briefly discuss how your business can expand its market presence, reach new customer segments, or diversify its product/service offerings for sustained growth.

7. Experienced Team:

Highlight key members of your team and their relevant experience. Investors often place importance on the competence of the leadership team. Briefly introduce key team members, emphasizing their qualifications and contributions to the business.

8. Financial Snapshot:

Provide a snapshot of your financial status. This could include key financial metrics, revenue figures, and profitability. A concise overview of your financial health gives investors a quick insight into the economic viability of your business.

9. Funding Requirements and Use of Funds:

If you're seeking funding, clearly state your funding requirements and how the funds will be utilized. This transparency demonstrates a strategic approach to resource allocation and aligns with the interests of potential investors.

10. Call to Action:

Conclude the overview with a strong call to action. Encourage investors and stakeholders to delve into the complete business plan for a more in-depth understanding of your business's potential and strategic direction.

By combining these elements, you create a concise yet powerful overview that hooks investors and stakeholders, prompting them to explore the details within the full business plan. Keep the language clear, engaging, and focused, ensuring that the overview serves as a compelling entry point to your business story.

* * *

CHAPTER 3: BUSINESS DESCRIPTION AND VISION

Providing A Detailed Description Of Your Business

Providing a detailed description of your business is essential in understanding the fundamentals of your venture.
Here's a guideline to get started:

Introduction to Your Business:

Begin by introducing your business with a concise overview. Provide the name of your company, its mission, and a brief statement encapsulating its core values.

Business Background and Origins:

Share the background and origins of your business. Explain how the idea for your venture originated, and highlight any key milestones or events that led to its establishment.

Nature of Your Business:

Clearly articulate the nature of your business. Describe the products or services you offer, and outline their unique features and benefits.
Define your industry and specify your target market.

Business Structure and Legal Status:

Detail the legal structure of your business, whether it's a sole proprietorship, partnership, LLC, corporation, or another form. Explain the reasoning behind your chosen structure.
Include information about your business's registration, licenses, and compliance with regulatory requirements.

Mission and Vision Statements:

Present your business's mission statement, outlining its fundamental purpose and the value it aims to deliver to customers.
Include a vision statement that reflects your long-term aspirations and goals for the business.

Core Values and Culture:

Define the core values that underpin your business culture. Discuss the principles and beliefs that guide decision-making within your organization.
Highlight any unique aspects of your company culture that set you apart.

Market Positioning:

Articulate your business's positioning within the market. Explain how you differentiate yourself from competitors and identify your competitive advantages.
Discuss factors such as pricing strategy, product differentiation, or unique selling propositions.

Business Location and Facilities:

Provide information about the physical location(s) of your business. Detail any facilities, offices, or production spaces.
Highlight the strategic significance of your chosen locations.

Key Personnel and Team Structure:

Introduce key personnel and members of your team. Briefly outline their roles, expertise, and contributions to the business.
Emphasize the qualifications and experience that make your team well-suited for success.

Company History and Milestones:

Share a brief history of your company, including significant milestones achieved over time.
Illustrate the growth and development of your business from its inception to the present.

Future Growth and Expansion:

Discuss your business's plans for future growth and expansion. Outline any strategies or initiatives you have in place to scale your operations.
Include a forward-looking perspective on the evolution of your business.

Partnerships and Collaborations:

Highlight any partnerships or collaborations that play a crucial role in your business. Explain how these relationships contribute to your overall success.
Showcase strategic alliances that enhance your business ecosystem.

By providing a comprehensive and original description of your business, you lay the foundation for a solid business plan. This section serves as a vital introduction, helping readers grasp the essence of your venture and setting the stage for the strategic planning that follows in your ebook.

Clarifying Your Business's Vision, Mission, And Values

Clarifying the vision, mission, and values of your business is a foundational step in defining the purpose and identity of your venture.

Define the Vision:

Begin by articulating the vision of your business. This is a forward-looking statement that encapsulates your aspirations and the ultimate impact you aim to achieve.
Communicate a compelling and inspiring picture of what success looks like for your business in the long term.

Craft the Mission Statement:

Develop a clear and concise mission statement that outlines the fundamental purpose of your business. Specify the products or services you provide and the value you offer to customers.
Emphasize the broader impact your business seeks to make on the market or community.

Identify Core Values:

Enumerate the core values that guide the decision-making and behavior within your business. These values represent the ethical principles and beliefs that form the foundation of your organizational culture.
Clearly articulate how these values shape the actions and relationships within your company.

Align Vision, Mission, and Values:

Ensure that there is alignment between your business's vision, mission, and values. Illustrate how each element contributes to a cohesive and

harmonious framework for your organization.
Highlight the synergy between your long-term vision, the day-to-day mission, and the underlying values that drive your business.

Incorporate Stakeholder Perspectives:

Consider the perspectives and interests of various stakeholders, including customers, employees, investors, and the community.
Demonstrate how your vision, mission, and values resonate with and address the needs of your diverse stakeholders.

Express Uniqueness and Differentiation:

Emphasize what makes your business unique and differentiates it from competitors. Showcase aspects of your vision, mission, and values that set you apart in the market.
Communicate the distinctive qualities that contribute to your competitive advantage.

Provide Examples and Stories:

Illustrate your business's vision, mission, and values with concrete examples and stories. Use anecdotes or case studies to bring these elements to life and make them relatable for readers.
Share instances where your business lived up to its values or achieved milestones aligned with the vision.

Emphasize Customer-Centricity:

Emphasize the customer-centric aspects of your mission and values.
Communicate how your business is dedicated to meeting customer needs, solving their problems, or enhancing their experiences.
Showcase customer testimonials or success stories that align with your business's mission.

Revisit and Revise:

Acknowledge that your vision, mission, and values may evolve over time. Emphasize the importance of revisiting and revising these elements to ensure they remain relevant and aligned with the changing landscape of your business.

Integrate Into Strategic Planning:

Emphasize the integration of your vision, mission, and values into the strategic planning process. Illustrate how these elements inform key decisions, goal-setting, and overall business strategy.

Showcase the practical application of your guiding principles in shaping the trajectory of your business.

By clarifying the vision, mission, and values of your business in an original and engaging manner, you lay a strong foundation for the development of a comprehensive business plan. This section serves as the guiding philosophy that informs strategic decisions and resonates with both internal and external stakeholders.

Outlining The Products Or Services You Offer

Introduction to Offerings:

Start by providing a concise introduction to your products or services. Clearly state what your business offers and the value it brings to customers.

Detailed Description:

Offer a detailed description of each product or service you provide. Highlight key features, specifications, or unique selling points that differentiate your offerings in the market.

Customer Benefits:

Emphasize the benefits your products or services bring to customers. Clearly articulate how your offerings address their needs, solve problems, or enhance their experiences.

Target Audience:

Specify your target audience for each product or service. Define the demographics, preferences, and characteristics of the customers you aim to serve.

Market Positioning:

Describe how your products or services are positioned in the market. Discuss your competitive advantage, pricing strategy, and any unique aspects that set you apart from competitors.

Product Life Cycle:

If applicable, discuss the life cycle of your products. Outline any plans for product updates, enhancements, or new releases in the future.

Technology and Innovation:

Highlight any technological aspects or innovations associated with your offerings. Showcase how your products or services leverage technology to provide a competitive edge.

Quality Assurance and Standards:

Address the quality assurance measures in place for your products or services. Discuss any industry standards, certifications, or quality control processes that ensure reliability and excellence.

Packaging and Presentation:

Discuss the packaging and presentation of your products. Explain how the visual and physical aspects contribute to the overall appeal and branding of your offerings.

Scalability and Expansion:

If applicable, touch upon the scalability of your offerings. Discuss plans for expansion, introducing new variants, or reaching additional markets with your products or services.

Customer Testimonials or Case Studies:

Include customer testimonials or case studies that highlight positive experiences with your products or services. Real-life examples add credibility and demonstrate the practical value of what you offer.

Regulatory Compliance:

Address any regulatory compliance requirements associated with your products or services. Ensure that your offerings meet industry standards and legal obligations.

Distribution Channels:

Explain the channels through which your products or services are distributed. Discuss partnerships, retail presence, online platforms, or any other avenues that facilitate customer access.

Customer Support and After-Sales Service:

Outline your approach to customer support and after-sales service. Emphasize your commitment to customer satisfaction and any policies in place for handling issues or inquiries.

Future Developments:

Conclude the section by briefly mentioning any future developments or plans for product/service enhancements. Highlight your business's adaptability and commitment to staying ahead in the market.

By presenting a comprehensive and original outline of your products or services in your business plan, you provide potential investors, stakeholders, and team members with a clear understanding of what your business brings to the market. This section serves as a crucial foundation for the overall strategic direction of your business.

* * *

CHAPTER 4: MARKET ANALYSIS AND INDUSTRY OVERVIEW

Conducting A Thorough Market Analysis

Conducting a thorough market analysis is a crucial step in creating a comprehensive business plan.

Introduction to Market Analysis:

Begin by introducing the importance of market analysis in your business plan. Emphasize that understanding the market is fundamental to making informed strategic decisions.

Define Your Target Market:

Clearly define your target market. Identify the demographics, psychographics, and characteristics of the customers you intend to serve. Provide a detailed description of your ideal customer persona.

Market Size and Growth Potential:

Estimate the overall size of your target market and its growth potential. Utilize available data, industry reports, or surveys to support your analysis. Highlight any trends or factors contributing to the market's growth.

Industry Overview:

Provide an overview of the industry in which your business operates. Discuss key players, market dynamics, and factors influencing the industry landscape.
Include relevant statistics and insights about the broader market context.

Competitive Landscape:

Analyze the competitive landscape. Identify direct and indirect competitors, their market share, strengths, weaknesses, and key differentiators.
Highlight your business's unique value proposition in comparison to competitors.

SWOT Analysis:

Conduct a SWOT analysis for your business. Evaluate its strengths, weaknesses, opportunities, and threats in relation to the market and competition.
Showcase how your strengths align with market opportunities.

Customer Needs and Preferences:

Explore customer needs and preferences within the market. Analyze consumer behavior, purchasing patterns, and any shifts in preferences.
Address how your products or services fulfill these needs.

Market Trends and Influences:

Identify current market trends and influences affecting your industry. Discuss technological advancements, cultural shifts, or regulatory changes that may impact your business.
Demonstrate your awareness of external factors shaping the market.

Regulatory Environment:

Address the regulatory environment relevant to your industry. Discuss any compliance requirements, licensing, or legal considerations that may affect

your business operations.
Emphasize your commitment to regulatory compliance.

Distribution Channels:

Examine the distribution channels in the market. Identify how products or services reach end-users, including retail, online platforms, partnerships, or other avenues.
Discuss your business's distribution strategy.

Price Analysis:

Conduct a pricing analysis within the market. Explore the pricing strategies of competitors and determine how your pricing aligns with perceived value.
Justify your pricing strategy based on market dynamics.

Market Entry Barriers:

Discuss any barriers to entry for new competitors in the market. Assess factors such as capital requirements, brand recognition, or regulatory hurdles.
Highlight how your business overcomes or leverages these barriers.

Customer Feedback and Surveys:

Include insights from customer feedback and surveys. Showcase testimonials, reviews, or findings from market research that validate your understanding of customer perceptions.
Demonstrate a customer-centric approach.

Sales and Marketing Strategies:

Outline your sales and marketing strategies based on your market analysis.
Detail how you plan to reach and engage your target audience.
Discuss promotional tactics, advertising channels, and customer acquisition plans.

Conclusion and Insights:

Conclude the market analysis section by summarizing key insights. Reiterate the significance of market understanding for your business strategy.

Emphasize your business's readiness to capitalize on identified opportunities and navigate challenges.

By conducting a thorough and original market analysis, you equip your business plan with valuable insights that inform strategic decisions. This section serves as a foundation for demonstrating your understanding of the market dynamics and positioning your business for success.

Identifying Target Markets And Customer Segments

Define Your Business Objectives:

Start by clearly defining your business objectives and goals. This sets the foundation for identifying target markets that align with your strategic vision.

Segmentation Criteria:

Establish criteria for customer segmentation. Consider demographics, psychographics, geographic location, and behavioral characteristics that are relevant to your industry.
Highlight the factors that will guide your segmentation strategy.

Primary Target Market:

Identify your primary target market. This is the core audience that is most likely to benefit from and engage with your products or services.
Provide a detailed profile of this primary customer segment.

Secondary Target Markets:

Acknowledge any secondary or niche markets that may also find value in your offerings. These segments could represent additional growth opportunities.
Clearly articulate the characteristics and needs of these secondary segments.

Customer Personas:

Create detailed customer personas for each target market. Develop fictional but representative profiles that encapsulate the typical traits, preferences, and behaviors of individuals in each segment.
Humanize your target audience to enhance understanding.

Needs and Pain Points:

Analyze the needs, challenges, and pain points of each customer segment.
Understand what motivates them to seek products or services like yours.
Demonstrate how your offerings address specific needs within each market.

Market Size and Potential:

Estimate the size and growth potential of each target market. Utilize market research, industry reports, or surveys to quantify the opportunities presented by each segment.
Discuss any trends or shifts that may impact market size.

Competitor Analysis by Segment:

Conduct a competitor analysis specific to each target market. Identify competitors catering to similar customer segments and assess their strengths and weaknesses.

Highlight how your business differentiates itself within each segment.

Unique Value Proposition for Each Segment:

Develop a unique value proposition tailored to each target market. Clearly communicate how your products or services meet the distinct needs and preferences of each segment.
Emphasize the specific benefits that set you apart.

Marketing Channels by Segment:

Outline the marketing channels and strategies you plan to employ for each target market. Consider the most effective ways to reach and engage individuals in each segment.
Tailor your messaging and promotional efforts to resonate with the characteristics of each market.

Customer Acquisition Strategies:

Detail customer acquisition strategies for each target market. Specify how you plan to attract and convert customers within each segment.
Discuss promotions, advertising, and other initiatives tailored to the preferences of each market.

Feedback Mechanisms:

Establish mechanisms for collecting feedback from each customer segment. Emphasize the importance of ongoing communication to understand evolving needs and preferences.
Showcase your commitment to customer-centric improvements.

Flexibility and Adaptability:

Acknowledge the potential for changes in the market landscape.
Demonstrate your business's flexibility and adaptability to evolving customer demands and industry trends.
Highlight strategies for staying responsive to market dynamics.

Metrics and Key Performance Indicators (KPIs):

Define metrics and KPIs relevant to each target market. Establish benchmarks for success and methods for tracking the performance of your marketing and sales efforts within each segment.
Illustrate your commitment to data-driven decision-making.

Conclusion:

Conclude the section by summarizing the importance of customer segmentation in your overall business strategy. Reiterate the unique value your business brings to each identified target market.
Emphasize your readiness to meet the diverse needs of customers across multiple segments.

By presenting a comprehensive and original approach to identifying target markets and customer segments, you demonstrate a deep understanding of your audience and set the stage for effective marketing and business development strategies. This section serves as a crucial component of your business plan, guiding your efforts to connect with and serve diverse customer groups.

Analyzing Industry Trends, Competitors, And Potential Challenges

Introduction to Industry Analysis:

Start with an introduction highlighting the significance of industry analysis in shaping your business strategy. Emphasize the dynamic nature of industries and the need for proactive planning.

Current Industry Trends:

Identify and analyze current trends within your industry. Explore technological advancements, consumer preferences, regulatory changes, and any other factors shaping the market landscape.
Discuss the implications of these trends on your business and highlight opportunities for innovation.

Future Industry Projections:

Discuss projections for the future of your industry. Utilize industry reports, market research, and expert opinions to anticipate potential shifts, growth areas, or emerging markets.
Showcase your business's forward-thinking approach in adapting to future industry dynamics.

Competitor Landscape:

Conduct a comprehensive analysis of the competitive landscape. Identify key competitors, their strengths, weaknesses, market share, and strategies. Emphasize your understanding of the competitive forces at play and how your business positions itself.

SWOT Analysis:

Perform a SWOT analysis for your business in relation to the industry. Evaluate internal strengths and weaknesses as well as external opportunities and threats.
Clearly communicate how you plan to leverage strengths and address weaknesses in the context of industry dynamics.

Market Entry Barriers:

Discuss any barriers to entry for new competitors in the industry. Examine factors such as capital requirements, regulatory compliance, brand recognition, or distribution networks.
Highlight your business's strategies for overcoming or leveraging these entry barriers.

Regulatory Environment:

Explore the regulatory environment relevant to your industry. Discuss any current or anticipated changes in regulations and their potential impact on your business operations.
Emphasize your commitment to compliance and any proactive measures taken to stay informed.

Potential Challenges and Risks:

Identify potential challenges and risks specific to your industry. Address factors such as economic downturns, supply chain disruptions, or technological obsolescence.
Outline risk mitigation strategies and contingency plans to demonstrate preparedness.

Innovation and Differentiation:

Showcase your business's commitment to innovation and differentiation. Discuss any unique approaches, proprietary technologies, or distinctive features that set your offerings apart from competitors.
Highlight how your business stays ahead in a rapidly evolving industry.

Customer Preferences and Feedback:

Analyze customer preferences within the industry. Utilize feedback, surveys, or market research to understand what customers value and seek in products or services.
Showcase your business's alignment with customer needs.

Supplier Relationships:

Discuss your relationships with suppliers and their significance to your industry. Evaluate the stability and reliability of your supply chain.
Emphasize strategies for maintaining strong supplier relationships and ensuring a consistent flow of resources.

Technology and Digital Transformation:

Explore the role of technology in your industry. Discuss how digital transformation or technological innovations may impact business operations, customer interactions, and overall industry dynamics. Highlight your business's adaptability to technological advancements.

Environmental and Social Trends:

Consider environmental and social trends relevant to your industry. Discuss sustainability practices, social responsibility, or any trends influencing consumer behavior.
Illustrate how your business aligns with or responds to these trends.

Conclusion:

Conclude the industry analysis section by summarizing key insights. Reiterate the strategic importance of understanding industry trends, competitors, and challenges in shaping your business plan.

Emphasize your business's readiness to navigate industry dynamics and capitalize on opportunities.

By presenting a comprehensive and original analysis of industry trends, competitors, and potential challenges, you showcase your business's strategic acumen and preparedness. This section serves as a crucial foundation for informed decision-making and proactive strategies to position your business for success in a dynamic market environment.

* * *

CHAPTER 5: ORGANIZATIONAL STRUCTURE AND MANAGEMENT

Defining Your Company's Organizational Structure

Introduction to Organizational Structure:

Begin with an introduction highlighting the importance of organizational structure in driving operational efficiency and achieving strategic goals. Emphasize that a well-defined structure provides clarity on roles and responsibilities within the company.

Type of Organizational Structure:

Clearly define the type of organizational structure your company adopts. Whether it's a hierarchical structure, flat organization, matrix structure, or a combination, explain the rationale behind your choice.
Discuss how the chosen structure aligns with your business goals and supports effective decision-making.

Leadership Team Overview:

Provide an overview of the leadership team within your organization.
Introduce key executives, founders, and decision-makers.
Briefly outline their roles, responsibilities, and contributions to the
company's success.

Departments and Functions:

Break down the organizational structure into departments and functions.
Define each department's specific role and the functions it performs within
the company.
Illustrate how departments collaborate to achieve overall business
objectives.

Reporting Lines and Hierarchy:

Outline the reporting lines and hierarchy within the organizational structure.
Clearly depict the chain of command and how information flows through
the organization.
Highlight any decentralized decision-making or cross-functional teams that
contribute to agility.

Roles and Responsibilities:

Define roles and responsibilities for key positions within the company.
Clearly articulate what each role entails, including tasks, decision-making
authority, and key performance indicators.
Emphasize the importance of role clarity in fostering accountability.

Team Collaboration and Communication:

Discuss how teams collaborate and communicate within the organizational
structure. Highlight any regular meetings, communication channels, or
collaborative tools used to enhance teamwork.
Showcase your commitment to fostering a culture of open communication.

Employee Development and Growth:

Address how employee development and growth are integrated into the organizational structure. Discuss training programs, mentorship opportunities, or career paths that support professional development. Illustrate how your organization invests in the growth of its employees.

Adaptability and Scalability:

Showcase the adaptability and scalability of your organizational structure. Discuss how it accommodates growth, changes in business needs, and emerging opportunities.
Illustrate instances where the structure has proven flexible in response to challenges.

Cultural Values and Alignment:

Emphasize the alignment of your organizational structure with the cultural values of your company. Discuss how the structure reflects and reinforces the core values that define your workplace culture.
Highlight the importance of cultural alignment in driving employee engagement.

Innovation and Cross-Functional Collaboration:

Discuss how your organizational structure fosters innovation and cross-functional collaboration. Highlight initiatives or structures that encourage the sharing of ideas and expertise across different departments.
Illustrate instances where cross-functional collaboration has led to innovative solutions.

Succession Planning:

Address succession planning within your organizational structure. Discuss strategies for identifying and developing internal talent to ensure a smooth transition in key roles.
Showcase your commitment to building a sustainable leadership pipeline.

Legal and Compliance Considerations:

Highlight any legal and compliance considerations associated with your organizational structure. Discuss adherence to labor laws, diversity and inclusion initiatives, and other regulatory requirements.
Illustrate your commitment to ethical business practices.

Conclusion:

Conclude the section by summarizing key points. Reiterate the role of the organizational structure in achieving business objectives and fostering a positive work environment.
Emphasize your company's commitment to a well-defined and adaptive organizational structure that contributes to long-term success.

By providing a comprehensive and original overview of your company's organizational structure, you showcase your understanding of the importance of organizational design in achieving strategic objectives. This section serves as a foundation for stakeholders to grasp the framework that supports your business operations and facilitates growth.

Introducing Key Team Members And Their Roles

Introduction to Key Team Members:

Begin with an introduction that emphasizes the importance of the team in driving the success of the business. Highlight the collaborative nature of the team and its role in achieving organizational goals.

Founder(s) and Leadership Team:

Introduce the founder(s) and key members of the leadership team. Provide a brief overview of their roles, responsibilities, and contributions to the

company's vision.
Emphasize their commitment to the business and its core values.

Biographical Information:

Include concise biographical information for each key team member.
Highlight their educational background, professional experience, and
notable achievements.
Use this section to convey the unique qualities and expertise each team
member brings to their role.

Roles and Responsibilities:

Clearly outline the roles and responsibilities of each key team member.
Define their specific contributions to the company's success and how their
roles align with overall business objectives.
Emphasize the complementary nature of the team's skill set.

Founder's Vision and Mission:

Discuss the founder's vision and mission for the company. Outline their
aspirations and the values that drive decision-making within the
organization.
Illustrate how the founder's vision influences the company's culture and
strategic direction.

CEO and Executive Team:

Introduce the CEO and members of the executive team. Highlight their
areas of expertise, leadership styles, and their collective role in steering the
company toward success.
Discuss the collaborative dynamics within the executive team.

Functional Heads and Departmental Leaders:

Introduce functional heads and leaders of different departments. Provide
insights into their specific responsibilities, the teams they oversee, and their

contributions to departmental goals.
Illustrate how each leader aligns with the overall organizational strategy.

Innovation and Research & Development (R&D):

Spotlight key team members involved in innovation and research & development. Discuss their roles in driving product development, creativity, and staying ahead in the market.
Showcase instances where their contributions have led to innovative solutions.

Marketing and Sales Team:

Introduce members of the marketing and sales teams. Highlight their roles in reaching target audiences, building brand awareness, and driving revenue.
Discuss strategies for customer acquisition and retention.

Operations and Supply Chain Management:

Introduce key members responsible for operations and supply chain management. Outline their roles in ensuring efficiency, quality control, and the smooth functioning of logistical processes.
Discuss strategies for optimizing operations and enhancing supply chain resilience.

Finance and Administration:

Introduce members of the finance and administration teams. Highlight their roles in financial management, budgeting, compliance, and overall administrative functions.
Discuss their contributions to maintaining fiscal health.
Human Resources and Talent Management:

Introduce the human resources and talent management team. Discuss their roles in recruitment, employee development, and fostering a positive workplace culture.

Highlight initiatives to attract and retain top talent.

Customer Support and Relationship Management:

Introduce members of the customer support and relationship management teams. Discuss their roles in ensuring customer satisfaction, handling inquiries, and building long-term relationships.
Showcase the team's commitment to exceptional customer service.

Collaborative Projects and Cross-Functional Teams:

Highlight instances of collaboration between key team members, cross-functional teams, and successful project outcomes. Illustrate the collaborative spirit that drives innovation and problem-solving.
Discuss the flexibility of the team in adapting to diverse challenges.

Conclusion:

Conclude the section by summarizing the collective strengths and contributions of the key team members. Reiterate their crucial roles in achieving the company's strategic objectives.
Emphasize the cohesion and synergy within the team that positions the company for success.

By providing a comprehensive and original introduction to key team members and their roles, you showcase the strength and capabilities of your leadership team. This section serves as a foundation for stakeholders to understand the collective expertise driving the company's success and innovation.

Outlining The Qualifications And Expertise Of Your Management Team

Introduction to Management Team:

Begin with an introduction that emphasizes the significance of a strong management team in driving business success. Highlight the team's role in executing the business strategy and achieving organizational goals.

Founders and Key Executives:

Introduce the founders and key executives of your company. Provide a brief overview of their backgrounds, roles, and contributions to the company. Emphasize the vision and values they bring to the leadership team.

Biographical Sketches:

Include biographical sketches for each member of the management team. Highlight key milestones, educational background, professional experience, and notable achievements.
Use this section to convey the unique expertise and skills each team member brings to the table.
Professional Experience:

Provide detailed information on the professional experience of each management team member. Outline their career progression, positions held, and specific accomplishments relevant to the industry.
Emphasize the depth and breadth of their experience.

Industry-Specific Expertise:

Highlight the industry-specific expertise of each team member. Discuss their knowledge of market trends, regulatory landscape, and insights gained through experience in the relevant sector.
Showcase how their expertise aligns with the needs of your business.

Educational Background:

Include details about the educational background of each team member. Highlight degrees, certifications, or specialized training that contributes to

their qualifications.
Emphasize how their academic achievements complement their professional expertise.

Leadership and Management Skills:

Discuss the leadership and management skills possessed by each team member. Highlight their ability to lead teams, make strategic decisions, and navigate challenges.
Illustrate instances where their leadership skills have positively impacted previous organizations.

Innovation and Problem-Solving Abilities:

Showcase the innovation and problem-solving abilities of your management team. Provide examples of how they have contributed to creative solutions, product development, or process improvements in their previous roles.
Illustrate their capacity to adapt and innovate in dynamic business environments.

Track Record of Success:

Present the track record of success for each team member. Discuss notable achievements, successful projects, or business milestones they have contributed to in their careers.
Use concrete metrics or case studies to quantify their impact.

Collaboration and Team Building:

Highlight the collaborative and team-building skills of your management team. Discuss their ability to foster a positive organizational culture, build cohesive teams, and encourage open communication.
Illustrate instances where they have successfully led and motivated teams.

Communication Skills:

Emphasize the communication skills of each team member. Discuss their ability to convey complex ideas, engage with stakeholders, and articulate the company's vision.
Illustrate how effective communication contributes to organizational alignment.

Strategic Vision and Decision-Making:

Discuss the strategic vision and decision-making capabilities of your management team. Highlight their ability to set long-term goals, make informed decisions, and steer the company toward success.
Showcase instances where their strategic vision has led to positive outcomes.

Customer Relationship Management:

Address the customer relationship management skills of your team. Discuss their approach to understanding and meeting customer needs, building client relationships, and ensuring customer satisfaction.
Illustrate instances where they have successfully managed client relations.

Commitment to Diversity and Inclusion:

Highlight the commitment of your management team to diversity and inclusion. Discuss any initiatives, policies, or values that demonstrate their dedication to creating an inclusive workplace.
Emphasize the importance of diverse perspectives in driving innovation.

Conclusion:

Conclude the section by summarizing the collective qualifications and expertise of your management team. Reiterate how their skills align with the strategic goals of the business.

Emphasize the confidence you have in your team's ability to lead the company to success.

By providing a comprehensive and original overview of your management team's qualifications and expertise, you showcase the strength of your leadership and build confidence in stakeholders. This section serves as a key component of your business plan, demonstrating the capabilities of your team and their readiness to navigate the challenges and opportunities ahead.

* * *

CHAPTER 6: PRODUCTS OR SERVICES OFFERED

Describing Your Products Or Services In Detail

When describing your products or services in a business plan, it's essential to convey uniqueness, value, and differentiation. Here are some steps and tips to help you describe your offerings in detail:

Understand Your Unique Selling Proposition (USP):

Identify what sets your products or services apart from competitors. Highlight features, benefits, and any proprietary elements that make your offerings unique.

Use Original Language:

Avoid copying text directly from competitors or existing materials. Develop your own wording that accurately represents your products or services.

Focus on Value Proposition:

Clearly articulate the value your products or services bring to customers. Emphasize how your offerings solve problems or meet specific needs.

Be Specific and Concrete:

Provide specific details about your products or services, such as features, specifications, or key attributes.
Use concrete examples to illustrate points.

Tell a Story:

Share the story behind your products or services. Explain the inspiration, development, or unique journey that led to their creation.
Storytelling can engage readers and make your offerings more memorable.

Highlight Benefits:

Clearly outline the benefits customers will derive from your products or services.
Explain how your offerings address pain points or enhance the lives of your target audience.

Avoid Generic Terms:

Steer clear of generic and overused phrases. Instead, use specific and descriptive language.
Define industry-specific terms if necessary, providing clarity for readers.

Use Analogies or Metaphors:

Analogies or metaphors can help readers grasp complex concepts more easily.
Relate your products or services to familiar experiences to enhance understanding.

Include Visuals:

If possible, incorporate visuals such as images, diagrams, or infographics to complement your written descriptions.
Visual elements can provide a clearer representation of your offerings.

Proofread and Edit:

Ensure your writing is clear, concise, and free of errors.
Proofread your content and consider seeking feedback to refine your descriptions.

Remember, the goal is to communicate effectively, showcase the uniqueness of your products or services, and build confidence in your business. Taking the time to craft original and compelling descriptions will help set your business plan apart.

Highlighting Unique Selling Propositions

When highlighting your unique selling propositions (USPs) in a business plan, it's crucial to communicate what sets your products or services apart from competitors while avoiding plagiarism. Here are some guidelines:

Identify Your USPs:

Clearly define what makes your products or services unique. Is it a specific feature, a particular aspect of your process, or a unique combination of elements?

Use Original Language:

Craft your own wording to describe your USPs. Avoid copying directly from competitors or industry sources.
Express the uniqueness in a way that aligns with your brand voice and values.

Focus on Value:

Emphasize how your USPs provide value to customers. Clearly articulate the benefits and advantages they offer.
Showcase how your unique features address customer needs or pain points.

Be Specific and Quantifiable:

Provide specific details and, if possible, quantify the advantages your USPs bring.
Use numbers, percentages, or other metrics to highlight the impact of your unique features.

Tell Your Story:

Share the backstory of your USPs. Explain the inspiration, development, or challenges overcome in creating these unique elements.
Storytelling adds authenticity and can help connect with your audience.

Differentiate from Competitors:

Explicitly mention how your USPs distinguish you from competitors in the market.
Highlight areas where your offerings excel and showcase a competitive edge.

Use Testimonials or Case Studies:

Incorporate customer testimonials or case studies that support your USPs.
Real-world examples can reinforce the credibility of your claims.
Ensure that any quoted content is used with permission.

Employ Visuals:

Use visuals, such as charts, graphs, or images, to illustrate the uniqueness of your products or services.
Visual representations can make complex information more digestible.

Avoid Generic Terms:

Steer clear of generic marketing buzzwords. Instead, use specific, descriptive language to convey the distinctiveness of your offerings. Clearly define terms unique to your industry or business.

Proofread and Revise:

Ensure your descriptions are clear, concise, and free of errors. Regularly review and update your USP descriptions to reflect any changes or enhancements.

By following these guidelines, you can effectively communicate your unique selling propositions in a way that stands out, showcases your strengths, and avoids any potential issues related to plagiarism.

Discussing The Development And Lifecycle Of Your Offerings

When discussing the development and lifecycle of your offerings in a business plan, it's important to provide a detailed yet original account of how your products or services came into existence, evolved, and continue to thrive.

Origins and Inspiration:

Begin by explaining the initial inspiration behind your products or services. Share the story of how the idea was conceived, and the problem or need it aimed to address.
Use your own words to describe the unique factors that motivated the development.

Development Process:

Outline the step-by-step process involved in developing your offerings.
Detail the research, design, testing, and any other key phases.
Avoid using verbatim text from external sources, and instead, express the
information in your own language.

Challenges and Solutions:

Discuss any challenges or obstacles faced during the development stage and
how your team overcame them. This adds authenticity to your narrative.
Use specific examples to illustrate problem-solving and innovation.
Milestones and Achievements:

Highlight significant milestones in the development journey. These could
include product launches, key partnerships, or technological breakthroughs.
Quantify achievements where possible, providing a sense of scale and
progress.

Customer Feedback and Iterations:

Incorporate customer feedback as a crucial element in the lifecycle. Discuss
how insights from users influenced product improvements and iterations.
Use testimonials or anonymized quotes to illustrate positive customer
experiences.

Market Adaptation:

Explain how your offerings have adapted to changes in the market or shifts
in customer preferences. Discuss any updates, enhancements, or
expansions.
Showcase your business's ability to stay relevant and responsive.

Product Lifecycle Stage:

Clearly define the current stage of your product or service lifecycle (e.g., introduction, growth, maturity, decline). This provides context for investors to understand where your offerings stand in the market.
Explain your strategies for sustaining or revitalizing the lifecycle.

Future Plans and Innovations:

Conclude by outlining your future plans for the offerings. Discuss potential innovations, expansions, or adaptations in response to emerging trends.
Use forward-looking language to convey a sense of vision and anticipation.

Proofread and Ensure Originality:

Carefully proofread your content to eliminate any unintentional similarities to existing texts.
Verify that your descriptions are unique and accurately represent your business journey.

By approaching the discussion of your offerings' development and lifecycle with authenticity and originality, you can effectively communicate the evolution of your products or services in a way that is compelling and avoids plagiarism concerns.

CHAPTER 7: MARKETING AND SALES STRATEGY

Developing A Comprehensive Marketing Plan

Developing a comprehensive marketing plan in a business document involves outlining your strategies for promoting your products or services, reaching your target audience, and achieving your business goals.

Understand Your Target Audience:

Begin by clearly defining your target market. Describe the demographics, psychographics, and behaviors of your ideal customers.
Use original language to explain why this audience is crucial to your business.
Market Analysis:

Conduct a thorough market analysis. Discuss industry trends, competitive landscape, and potential opportunities or challenges.
Use your own observations and insights, avoiding direct copying from external sources.

SWOT Analysis:

Conduct a SWOT analysis (Strengths, Weaknesses, Opportunities, Threats) specific to your business. Discuss internal and external factors that impact your marketing strategy.

Express your unique perspective on your business's strengths and weaknesses.

Clear Objectives:

Clearly state your marketing objectives. What do you aim to achieve with your marketing efforts? Ensure your goals are specific, measurable, achievable, relevant, and time-bound (SMART).
Use original language to outline your specific business goals.

Marketing Strategies:

Detail your marketing strategies. Include a mix of online and offline tactics such as social media, content marketing, SEO, advertising, events, etc. Explain why each strategy is relevant to your business, and use your own words to describe their implementation.

Budget Allocation:

Provide a breakdown of your marketing budget. Specify how much you plan to allocate to each marketing channel or strategy.
Use original language to justify your budget allocations based on your business needs.

Timeline and Milestones:

Create a timeline for the implementation of your marketing strategies. Include key milestones and deadlines.
Express the progression of your plan in a way that is unique to your business.

Metrics and KPIs:

Define the key performance indicators (KPIs) and metrics you will use to measure the success of your marketing efforts.
Use original language to explain why these metrics are relevant to tracking your business's performance.

Risk Assessment:

Discuss potential risks and challenges associated with your marketing plan.
Detail contingency plans or strategies to mitigate these risks.
Use original language to address the unique risks your business may face.

Integration with Overall Business Strategy:

Emphasize how your marketing plan aligns with your overall business
strategy. Demonstrate the coherence between marketing goals and broader
business objectives.
Use original language to articulate the synergy between marketing and
business strategies.

Proofread and Citation:

Ensure that your writing is clear, concise, and free of errors.
If you need to include specific data or information from external sources,
cite them appropriately using a recognized citation style.

*By focusing on originality, clarity, and specificity, you can create a
comprehensive marketing plan that effectively communicates your
strategies without the risk of plagiarism. Always use your unique
business context and language to showcase the distinctiveness of
your marketing approach.*

Outlining Sales Strategies And Tactics

Outlining sales strategies and tactics in a business plan involves detailing how your business plans to generate revenue, reach customers, and achieve sales goals. Here's a guide on how to articulate your sales plan:

Clearly Define Sales Objectives:

Begin by clearly stating your sales objectives. What specific targets do you aim to achieve? Make sure your objectives are measurable and aligned with your overall business goals.
Express these objectives in your own words, avoiding direct copying from external sources.

Identify Target Customer Segments:

Clearly identify and describe your target customer segments. Discuss the demographics, psychographics, and behaviors of your ideal customers.
Use original language to explain why these customer segments are crucial to your sales strategy.

Sales Channels:

Outline the various sales channels you plan to utilize, whether they are direct sales, e-commerce, partnerships, or a combination of approaches.
Provide your own perspective on why each channel is appropriate for your business.

Sales Team Structure:

Detail the structure of your sales team, including roles and responsibilities.
Discuss how the team is organized and how it supports your sales strategies.
Use original language to describe your team structure and dynamics.

Customer Relationship Management (CRM):

Discuss how you will manage customer relationships throughout the sales process. Mention any CRM tools or strategies you plan to implement.

Use original language to explain how your CRM approach is tailored to your business.

Sales Funnel:

Explain the stages of your sales funnel, from lead generation to conversion. Discuss how you plan to move prospects through each stage.

Use your own words to describe the unique aspects of your sales funnel.

Sales Tactics and Techniques:

Detail the specific tactics and techniques your sales team will employ to engage and convert leads. This could include personalized selling, content marketing, upselling, etc.
Use original language to explain how these tactics align with your business objectives.

Pricing Strategy:

Outline your pricing strategy. Explain how you arrived at your pricing model and how it aligns with the value you offer to customers.
Use original language to justify your pricing decisions.

Sales Forecast:

Provide a realistic sales forecast based on your market research and historical data. Explain the assumptions and factors influencing your projections.
Express your business's unique sales forecast without copying from external sources.

Training and Development:

Discuss any training and development programs in place to enhance the skills of your sales team. Explain how ongoing learning contributes to your sales success.
Use original language to describe your commitment to continuous improvement.

Proofread and Citation:

Ensure your writing is clear, concise, and free of errors.
If you need to include specific data or information from external sources, cite them appropriately using a recognized citation style.

By focusing on originality, specificity, and a clear understanding of your business context, you can create a compelling and unique outline of your sales strategies and tactics in your business plan. Always use your own language to express the distinctiveness of your approach.

Setting Sales Targets And Forecasting Revenue

Setting sales targets and forecasting revenue in a business plan is crucial for outlining your financial expectations and demonstrating the viability of your business:

Clearly Define Sales Targets:

Begin by clearly defining your sales targets. Specify the volume of products or services you aim to sell within a given timeframe.

Use your own words to express these targets, avoiding direct copying from external sources.

Basis for Setting Targets:

Explain the rationale behind your chosen sales targets. Discuss market research, industry trends, and customer demand that informed your decisions.

Use original language to describe the factors influencing your target-setting process.

Segmented Targets:

If applicable, set segmented sales targets for different customer segments, product lines, or geographic regions. Tailor your approach based on the diversity of your offerings.

Use your unique business context to explain the rationale behind segmented targets.

Sales Velocity and Conversion Rates:

Discuss the sales velocity and conversion rates you expect. Explain how quickly leads move through your sales funnel and the percentage that convert into customers.
Use original language to articulate your expectations for sales velocity and conversion rates.

Revenue Forecasting:

Provide a detailed revenue forecast, outlining the expected income over a specified period. Break down the forecast by product, service, or any relevant category.
Use your own words to explain the assumptions and methodologies used in your revenue forecasting.

Pricing Assumptions:

Explain any pricing assumptions or changes that influenced your revenue forecast. Discuss how alterations in pricing may impact sales volume and overall revenue.
Use original language to describe the considerations behind your pricing decisions.

Market Trends and External Factors:

Discuss how market trends and external factors may impact your sales targets and revenue forecasts. Address any potential risks or opportunities arising from the external environment.

Use your own language to describe the market dynamics affecting your business.

Historical Performance and Benchmarking:

If applicable, include historical sales data and benchmarking against industry standards. Showcase your business's growth trajectory and how it aligns with your future targets.

Use original language to explain your business's unique journey and positioning.

Assumptions and Risks:

Clearly outline the assumptions made in your sales targets and revenue forecasts. Discuss potential risks and how you plan to mitigate them.

Use original language to express the unique considerations and risk mitigation strategies for your business.

Proofread and Citation:

Ensure your writing is clear, concise, and free of errors.
If you need to include specific data or information from external sources, cite them appropriately using a recognized citation style.

By focusing on originality, specificity, and a thorough understanding of your business context, you can create a robust section on setting sales targets and forecasting revenue in your business plan. Always use your unique language to convey the distinctiveness of your sales projections.

* * *

CHAPTER 8: FUNDING REQUEST AND FINANCIAL PROJECTIONS

Detailing Your Funding Requirements And How Funds Will Be Used

Detailing funding requirements and how funds will be used in a business plan is essential for communicating your financial needs and demonstrating a clear plan for resource allocation:

Outline Funding Requirements:

Begin by clearly stating your funding requirements. Specify the amount of capital needed to launch or grow your business.
Express these requirements in your own words, avoiding direct copying from external sources.

Justify Funding Needs:

Provide a rationale for your funding requirements. Explain how the capital will be used to achieve specific business objectives, such as product development, marketing, or expansion.

Use original language to describe the strategic importance of the funds to your business.

Breakdown of Fund Usage:

Break down how the funds will be allocated across different aspects of your business. This could include categories such as product development, marketing, operations, and working capital.

Use your own words to explain the allocation strategy and the reasoning behind each category.

Cost Estimates:

Provide detailed cost estimates for each aspect of your business plan. Include quotes, bids, or market research data to support your estimates.

Use original language to describe the cost breakdown and ensure accuracy in your calculations.

Timeline for Fund Usage:

Outline the timeline for fund usage. Specify when and how the funds will be disbursed over the course of your business's development or growth.

Use your unique business context to describe the timeline for fund utilization.

Risk Assessment:

Discuss potential risks associated with fund usage and how you plan to mitigate them. Address any uncertainties or challenges that may impact your ability to achieve your funding objectives.

Use original language to describe the unique risks and mitigation strategies for your business.

Alternative Funding Sources:

Explore alternative funding sources beyond the primary funding requirement. Discuss options such as loans, grants, investment partnerships, or crowdfunding.

Use your own words to explain the potential benefits and drawbacks of each funding source.

Financial Projections:

Provide financial projections that illustrate the impact of the funding on your business's performance. Include forecasts for revenue, expenses, and cash flow based on different funding scenarios.
Use original language to describe your financial projections and assumptions.

Exit Strategy (if applicable):

If seeking investment, discuss potential exit strategies for investors. Explain how investors can expect to realize returns on their investment, whether through acquisition, IPO, or other means.

Use your own language to describe the exit strategy options and their implications.

Proofread and Citation:

Ensure your writing is clear, concise, and free of errors.
If you need to include specific data or information from external sources, cite them appropriately using a recognized citation style.

By focusing on originality, specificity, and a thorough understanding of your business's financial needs, you can create a compelling section on detailing funding requirements and how funds will be used in your business plan. Always use your unique language to convey the distinctiveness of your financial strategy.

Providing Financial Projections, Including Income Statements, Balance Sheets, And Cash Flow Forecasts

When providing financial projections, including income statements, balance sheets, and cash flow forecasts in a business plan, it's essential to present accurate, realistic, and original data to demonstrate the financial viability of your venture. Here's a guide on how to articulate this section while ensuring originality and avoiding plagiarism:

Gather Relevant Data:

Begin by gathering all relevant financial data, including historical financial statements (if applicable), sales forecasts, expense estimates, and any other pertinent information.

Use your own data and insights, avoiding direct copying from external sources.

Income Statement (Profit and Loss Statement):

Present your projected income statement, detailing revenue, expenses, and net income over a specific period (typically monthly or annually).
Use original language to describe the revenue sources and expense categories contributing to your projected profitability.

Balance Sheet:

Provide a projected balance sheet, outlining your business's assets, liabilities, and equity at a specific point in time.
Use your own words to describe the composition of assets, liabilities, and equity, and ensure accuracy in your projections.

Cash Flow Forecast:

Develop a cash flow forecast, detailing the expected cash inflows and outflows over a defined period. Include operating activities, investing activities, and financing activities.
Use original language to describe the sources and uses of cash within your business operations.

Assumptions and Methodology:

Clearly outline the assumptions and methodologies used to create your financial projections. Explain the basis for your revenue forecasts, expense estimates, and other key financial metrics.
Use your own language to describe the rationale behind your assumptions and methodologies.

Sensitivity Analysis:

Conduct sensitivity analysis to assess the potential impact of changes in key variables on your financial projections. Discuss how variations in factors such as sales volume, pricing, or operating expenses may affect your bottom line.
Use original language to describe the sensitivity analysis and its implications for your financial outlook.

Risk Assessment:

Discuss potential risks and uncertainties that may impact your financial projections. Address factors such as market volatility, regulatory changes, or competitive pressures.

Use original language to describe the specific risks and mitigation strategies for your business.

Financial Ratios and Metrics:

Include relevant financial ratios and metrics to provide additional context for your projections. This could include metrics such as gross margin, net profit margin, return on investment (ROI), and others.

Use your own language to explain the significance of these ratios and metrics in evaluating your business's financial health.

Formatting and Presentation:

Present your financial projections in a clear, organized format that is easy to understand. Use tables, charts, and graphs to visually illustrate key data points.

Ensure that your formatting is consistent and professional throughout the financial projections section.

Proofread and Citation:

Ensure your writing is clear, concise, and free of errors.
If you need to include specific data or information from external sources, cite them appropriately using a recognized citation style.

By focusing on originality, accuracy, and transparency in your financial projections, you can effectively demonstrate the financial feasibility of your business venture without the risk of plagiarism. Always use your unique data, insights, and language to convey the distinctiveness of your financial outlook.

Demonstrating The Potential Return On Investment For Investors

When demonstrating the potential return on investment (ROI) for investors in a business plan, it's crucial to provide a clear and compelling financial analysis that showcases the profitability and growth potential of your venture:

Executive Summary of ROI:

Begin by summarizing the potential return on investment for investors in a concise and compelling manner. Highlight key financial metrics such as projected ROI, payback period, and internal rate of return (IRR).
Use original language to capture the essence of your investment opportunity and its attractiveness to potential investors.

Financial Projections:

Provide detailed financial projections that illustrate the potential ROI for investors. Include income statements, balance sheets, and cash flow forecasts over multiple years.
Use your own data and assumptions to create the financial projections, avoiding direct copying from external sources.

Profitability Analysis:

Conduct a profitability analysis to showcase the potential earnings and margins of your business. Highlight factors driving profitability, such as pricing strategy, cost management, and revenue growth.
Use original language to describe the profitability drivers and their impact on the bottom line.

Market Opportunity Assessment:

Present a thorough assessment of the market opportunity for your business. Discuss market size, growth trends, competitive landscape, and potential market share.
Use original language to articulate the market opportunity and the potential for revenue growth.

Competitive Advantage:

Highlight your business's competitive advantage and differentiation factors that contribute to its potential ROI. Discuss unique features, proprietary technology, strong brand presence, or other factors that set your business apart.
Use your own words to describe the competitive advantage and its significance in driving investor returns.

Risk Mitigation Strategies:

Address potential risks and uncertainties that may impact investor ROI. Discuss mitigation strategies and contingency plans to minimize risk exposure.
Use original language to describe the specific risks and mitigation strategies for your business.

Exit Strategy (if applicable):

Outline potential exit strategies for investors to realize returns on their investment. Discuss options such as acquisition, IPO, or strategic partnerships.
Use your own language to describe the exit strategy options and their implications for investor ROI.

Investment Terms and Structure:

Clearly define the investment terms and structure, including equity stake, valuation, investment amount, and expected returns. Provide transparency and clarity to potential investors.
Use original language to describe the investment terms and structure in a way that is clear and understandable.

Scenario Analysis:

Conduct scenario analysis to assess the potential impact of different market conditions on investor ROI. Explore best-case, worst-case, and base-case

scenarios to provide a comprehensive view of potential outcomes.
Use original language to describe the scenario analysis and its implications for investor decision-making.

Proofread and Citation:

Ensure your writing is clear, concise, and free of errors.
If you need to include specific data or information from external sources, cite them appropriately using a recognized citation style.

By focusing on originality, transparency, and thorough financial analysis, you can effectively demonstrate the potential return on investment for investors in your business plan without the risk of plagiarism. Always use your unique data, insights, and language to convey the attractiveness of your investment opportunity.

* * *

CHAPTER 9: OPERATIONS PLAN

Describing Day-To-Day Operations

When describing day-to-day operations in a business plan, it's important to provide a detailed yet original account of how your business will function on a daily basis:

Outline Key Activities:

Begin by outlining the key activities involved in your day-to-day operations. This could include production processes, service delivery, customer interactions, administrative tasks, etc.

Use your own words to describe the specific activities that are essential to running your business smoothly.
Staffing and Organizational Structure:

Describe the staffing requirements and organizational structure of your business. Outline the roles and responsibilities of each team member and how they contribute to daily operations.

Use original language to explain the unique dynamics of your team and organizational hierarchy.

Workflow and Processes:

Detail the workflow and processes that govern your day-to-day operations.
Discuss how tasks are assigned, executed, and monitored to ensure
efficiency and quality.
Use your own words to describe the specific workflows and processes
tailored to your business needs.

Technology and Tools:

Discuss the technology and tools utilized in your day-to-day operations.
This could include software systems, equipment, machinery, or other
resources necessary to perform tasks.

Use original language to explain how technology and tools are integrated
into your operations to enhance productivity and effectiveness.

Quality Control and Assurance:

Explain the quality control and assurance measures implemented in your
operations. Discuss how you ensure consistency, accuracy, and compliance
with standards or regulations.

Use your unique business context to describe the specific quality control
processes in place.

Customer Interaction and Service Delivery:

Describe how you interact with customers on a day-to-day basis and deliver
your products or services. Discuss communication channels, customer
service protocols, and order fulfillment processes.

Use original language to convey the customer-centric approach and
personalized service delivery of your business.

Inventory Management and Supply Chain:

Outline your inventory management practices and supply chain processes.
Discuss how you procure materials, manage inventory levels, and fulfill

orders in a timely manner.

Use your own words to describe the intricacies of your inventory management and supply chain strategy.

Safety and Compliance:

Address safety protocols and regulatory compliance requirements relevant to your operations. Discuss how you ensure a safe working environment for employees and adhere to legal obligations.

Use original language to describe your commitment to safety and compliance standards.

Continuous Improvement:

Highlight your approach to continuous improvement in day-to-day operations. Discuss how you identify areas for optimization, implement changes, and measure outcomes.

Use your own language to describe the culture of continuous improvement within your organization.
Proofread and Citation:

Ensure your writing is clear, concise, and free of errors.
If you need to include specific data or information from external sources, cite them appropriately using a recognized citation style.

By emphasizing originality, specificity, and a comprehensive grasp of your business operations, you have the opportunity to craft an engaging portrayal of your day-to-day activities within your business plan. Ensure to employ your distinct language consistently to highlight the uniqueness of your operational processes.

Detailing Manufacturing Processes, If Applicable

Detailing manufacturing processes in a business plan involves providing a comprehensive and original description of how your products are produced, assembled, and delivered, if applicable:

Overview of Manufacturing Process:

Begin by providing an overview of your manufacturing process, explaining the steps involved from raw materials to finished products.

Use your own words to describe the unique aspects of your manufacturing process.

Materials and Inputs:

Detail the materials and inputs required for manufacturing your products. Discuss the sourcing, procurement, and handling of raw materials, components, or ingredients.
Use original language to describe the specific materials used in your manufacturing process and their sources.

Production Flow and Sequence:

Outline the production flow and sequence of operations in your manufacturing process. Discuss how materials are transformed at each stage and the order in which tasks are performed.

Use your unique business context to describe the production flow and sequence tailored to your operations.

Equipment and Machinery:

Describe the equipment, machinery, and tools used in your manufacturing process. Discuss their functions, capabilities, and maintenance requirements.
Use original language to explain how the equipment and machinery are utilized to optimize production efficiency.

Quality Control Measures:

Explain the quality control measures implemented throughout the manufacturing process. Discuss inspection checkpoints, testing procedures, and quality assurance protocols.

Use your own words to describe the specific quality control measures in place to ensure product quality and consistency.

Workforce and Skills:

Discuss the workforce required for your manufacturing operations. Outline the roles and skills of employees involved in production, assembly, quality control, and maintenance.

Use original language to describe the expertise and capabilities of your workforce.
Safety Protocols:

Address safety protocols and procedures relevant to your manufacturing operations. Discuss measures in place to ensure a safe working environment for employees and compliance with regulatory standards.

Use your own language to describe your commitment to safety and adherence to safety regulations.

Efficiency Improvement Strategies:

Highlight strategies for improving efficiency and productivity in your manufacturing process. Discuss initiatives such as lean manufacturing, automation, or process optimization.

Use original language to describe how you continually seek to enhance efficiency in your operations.
Environmental Considerations:

Discuss any environmental considerations or sustainability initiatives incorporated into your manufacturing process. Address efforts to minimize waste, conserve resources, and reduce environmental impact.

Use your own words to describe your commitment to environmental responsibility.

Proofread and Citation:

Ensure your writing is clear, concise, and free of errors.
If you need to include specific data or information from external sources, cite them appropriately using a recognized citation style.

By focusing on originality, specificity, and a thorough understanding of your manufacturing processes, you can create a compelling description in your business plan without the risk of plagiarism. Always use your unique language to convey the distinctiveness of your manufacturing operations.

Addressing Logistics, Technology, And Other Operational Aspects

When addressing logistics, technology, and other operational aspects in a business plan, it's essential to provide a detailed and original description of how these components contribute to the efficiency and effectiveness of your business operations:

Logistics Management:

Begin by detailing your logistics management approach. Discuss how you handle inventory, transportation, warehousing, and distribution to ensure timely delivery of products or services.

Use original language to describe your logistics strategy and any unique features tailored to your business needs.

Supply Chain Integration:

Explain how your business integrates with suppliers, distributors, and other partners within the supply chain. Discuss collaboration, coordination, and communication strategies to streamline operations.

Use your unique business context to describe the integration of your supply chain partners and the benefits it brings.

Technology Infrastructure:

Detail the technology infrastructure supporting your operations. Discuss software systems, IT networks, and hardware equipment used to manage processes, data, and communication.

Use original language to explain how technology is leveraged to enhance operational efficiency and decision-making.

Data Management and Analytics:

Discuss your approach to data management and analytics. Explain how you collect, analyze, and utilize data to inform strategic decisions, optimize processes, and improve performance.

Use your own words to describe the data management and analytics practices tailored to your business requirements.

Automation and Robotics:

Address any automation and robotics technologies employed in your operations. Discuss how these technologies are utilized to streamline production, reduce labor costs, and enhance precision.

Use original language to describe the integration of automation and robotics into your operations and the resulting efficiencies gained.

Quality Management Systems:

Explain your quality management systems and processes. Discuss standards, certifications, and procedures in place to ensure product or service quality, consistency, and customer satisfaction.

Use your own language to describe the quality management systems unique to your business and their impact on operational excellence.

Risk Management Strategies:

Discuss your risk management strategies for mitigating operational risks. Address factors such as supply chain disruptions, technological failures, cybersecurity threats, and regulatory compliance.

Use original language to describe your risk management approach and the measures taken to safeguard your business operations.

Continuous Improvement Initiatives:

Highlight continuous improvement initiatives embedded in your operations. Discuss methodologies such as Lean, Six Sigma, or Kaizen, and initiatives to foster innovation and adaptability.

Use your unique business context to describe the culture of continuous improvement within your organization.

Environmental and Social Responsibility:

Address any environmental and social responsibility initiatives integrated into your operations. Discuss efforts to reduce environmental impact, promote sustainability, and contribute positively to society.

Use original language to describe your commitment to environmental and social responsibility and the initiatives undertaken to fulfill these commitments.

Proofread and Citation:

Ensure your writing is clear, concise, and free of errors.
If you need to include specific data or information from external sources, cite them appropriately using a recognized citation style.

By focusing on originality, specificity, and a thorough understanding of your operational aspects, you can create a compelling description in your business plan without the risk of plagiarism. Always use your unique language to convey the distinctiveness of your operational strategies and capabilities.

* * *

CHAPTER 10: RISK ANALYSIS AND MITIGATION

Identifying Potential Risks And Challenges

When identifying potential risks and challenges associated with creating a business plan ebook, it's crucial to assess various aspects of the process comprehensively. Here's a guide on how to articulate this without plagiarizing:

Content Development Risks:

Consider potential challenges related to content development, such as ensuring accuracy, relevance, and coherence of the information presented. Discuss the risk of incomplete or outdated information and the need for thorough research and fact-checking.
Formatting and Design Challenges:

Address challenges related to formatting and design, including the selection of appropriate templates, fonts, colors, and layouts.
Discuss the risk of inconsistency in design elements and the importance of maintaining a professional and visually appealing presentation.
Copyright and Plagiarism Concerns:

Highlight the risk of copyright infringement and plagiarism when using third-party content, images, or graphics.
Emphasize the importance of obtaining proper permissions, licenses, or attributions to avoid legal issues and maintain integrity.

Technical Issues:

Identify potential technical challenges, such as software compatibility issues, file format conversions, and ebook distribution platforms' requirements.
Discuss the risk of formatting errors, glitches, or accessibility issues that may affect the readability and usability of the ebook.
Market Research and Audience Analysis:

Consider risks associated with market research and audience analysis, such as inaccurate target audience identification or misinterpretation of market trends.
Discuss the risk of creating content that does not resonate with the intended audience or fails to address their needs and preferences effectively.
Competition and Market Saturation:

Assess the risk of competition and market saturation in the ebook publishing industry. Consider the challenges of standing out among existing offerings and attracting readership.
Discuss strategies for differentiation, branding, and marketing to mitigate the risk of being overshadowed by competitors.
Resource Constraints:

Acknowledge resource constraints, such as time, budget, and expertise, that may impact the quality and scope of the business plan ebook.
Discuss the risk of overcommitting or underestimating resource requirements and the importance of realistic planning and prioritization.
Distribution and Promotion Challenges:

Consider challenges related to ebook distribution and promotion, including visibility on online platforms, competition for reader attention, and marketing effectiveness.
Discuss the risk of low sales or limited reach and the need for strategic promotion, partnerships, and advertising to maximize exposure and sales potential.
Feedback and Iteration Process:

Address the risk of receiving negative feedback or criticism from readers, stakeholders, or reviewers.
Emphasize the importance of maintaining an open-minded approach, actively soliciting feedback, and iteratively improving the ebook based on constructive criticism.
Legal and Regulatory Compliance:

Highlight risks related to legal and regulatory compliance, such as privacy laws, data protection regulations, and intellectual property rights.
Discuss the risk of non-compliance penalties or legal disputes and the importance of conducting thorough legal reviews and adhering to relevant laws and regulations.

Contingency Planning:

Propose contingency plans and risk mitigation strategies for addressing potential challenges identified throughout the ebook creation process.

Discuss the importance of flexibility, adaptability, and resilience in responding to unexpected obstacles and setbacks.

By addressing these potential risks and challenges in an original and comprehensive manner, you can demonstrate a thorough understanding of the ebook creation process and your preparedness to navigate potential obstacles effectively.

Developing A Risk Mitigation And Contingency Plan

Identify Risks: Start by identifying potential risks that could impact your business. These could include market risks, financial risks, operational risks, legal risks, etc.

Assess Risks: Evaluate the likelihood and potential impact of each risk. Prioritize risks based on their severity and likelihood of occurrence.

Develop Mitigation Strategies: Develop strategies to mitigate or reduce the impact of identified risks. This could include diversifying your revenue streams, implementing security measures, or obtaining insurance.

Create Contingency Plans: Develop contingency plans for managing risks that cannot be fully mitigated. Identify alternative courses of action that can be taken if a risk materializes.

Allocate Resources: Allocate resources, such as budget, personnel, and time, to implement risk mitigation and contingency plans.

Test and Review: Regularly test your risk mitigation and contingency plans to ensure they are effective. Review and update your plans as needed based on changing circumstances.

Communicate and Train: Ensure that your team is aware of the risk mitigation and contingency plans and understands their roles and responsibilities. Provide training if necessary.

Monitor and Adjust: Continuously monitor the effectiveness of your risk mitigation and contingency plans. Be prepared to adjust your plans based on new information or changing circumstances.

Document Everything: Document your risk mitigation and contingency plans, including the identified risks, mitigation strategies, and contingency plans. Keep this documentation updated and easily accessible.

By developing a comprehensive risk mitigation and contingency plan, you can better prepare your business to manage and overcome

Assuring Investors Of Your Ability To Navigate Uncertainties

Thoroughly Understand Your Market: Demonstrate a deep understanding of your target market, including trends, customer needs, and competitive landscape. This shows investors that you are well-informed and prepared to adapt to changes.

Highlight Your Team's Expertise: Showcase the expertise and experience of your team members. Highlight any relevant skills, qualifications, or past successes that demonstrate your ability to navigate uncertainties.

Provide a Detailed Business Plan: Present a detailed and well-thought-out business plan that outlines your strategies for dealing with uncertainties. Include contingency plans and risk mitigation strategies to show that you have considered potential challenges.

Demonstrate Flexibility: Show that you are flexible and able to adapt to changing circumstances. Discuss how you will monitor market changes and adjust your strategies accordingly.

Focus on Strong Financial Management: Emphasize your commitment to strong financial management practices. Provide financial projections and explain how you will manage cash flow and expenses during uncertain times.

Showcase Past Successes: If applicable, highlight any past successes or milestones that demonstrate your ability to navigate uncertainties. This could include surviving economic downturns or successfully launching new products in competitive markets.

Provide Transparent Communication: Be open and transparent with investors about the risks and uncertainties facing your business. Provide regular updates and communicate any changes to your plans or strategies.

Seek Strategic Partnerships: Consider forming strategic partnerships or alliances that can help you navigate uncertainties. This could include partnerships with suppliers, distributors, or other businesses in your industry.

By following these steps, you can assure investors of your ability to navigate uncertainties and increase their confidence in your business.

* * *

CHAPTER 11: IMPLEMENTATION TIMELINE AND MILESTONES

Creating A Realistic Implementation Timeline

Creating a realistic implementation timeline for a business plan involves several key steps:

Define Your Goals: Start by clearly defining your business goals and objectives. These should be specific, measurable, achievable, relevant, and time-bound (SMART goals).

Identify Key Tasks: Break down your goals into smaller, actionable tasks. Identify the key activities that need to be completed to achieve each goal.

Sequence Tasks: Determine the order in which tasks need to be completed. Some tasks may be dependent on others, so it's important to establish a logical sequence.

Estimate Timeframes: Estimate the time it will take to complete each task. Be realistic in your estimates and consider factors such as resources, dependencies, and potential obstacles.

Allocate Resources: Identify the resources (e.g., personnel, equipment, funds) needed to complete each task. Ensure that resources are allocated efficiently and effectively.

Create a Timeline: Use a timeline format (e.g., Gantt chart) to map out the sequence of tasks and their estimated durations. This will help you visualize the timeline and identify any potential bottlenecks or overlapping tasks.

Monitor and Adjust: Regularly review your implementation timeline to track progress and make any necessary adjustments. Be flexible and prepared to modify your timeline as needed to stay on track.

Communicate and Coordinate: Keep your team informed about the implementation timeline and ensure that everyone is clear on their roles and responsibilities. Encourage open communication and collaboration to ensure a smooth implementation process.

By following these steps, you can create a realistic implementation timeline that will help you effectively execute your business plan and achieve your goals.

Setting Milestones To Track Progress

Setting milestones to track progress is crucial for monitoring the implementation of your business plan. Here's how you can do it:

Review Your Goals: Start by reviewing the goals you've set in your business plan. Break down each goal into smaller, more manageable milestones.

Make Them Specific: Each milestone should be specific, measurable, achievable, relevant, and time-bound (SMART). This makes it easier to track progress and evaluate success.

Set Clear Deadlines: Assign deadlines to each milestone to create a sense of urgency and keep your team focused on achieving them.

Prioritize: Identify the most critical milestones that are key to the success of your business. Focus on achieving these first before moving on to less critical ones.

Track Progress: Regularly track your progress towards each milestone. Use metrics and key performance indicators (KPIs) to measure progress objectively.

Celebrate Achievements: When you reach a milestone, celebrate the achievement with your team. This helps boost morale and motivation.

Adjust as Needed: Be flexible and willing to adjust your milestones if circumstances change. Sometimes, unforeseen challenges or opportunities may require you to modify your plan.

Communicate: Keep your team informed about the milestones and progress. Encourage open communication and collaboration to ensure everyone is aligned towards the same goals.

By setting clear, achievable milestones and tracking progress regularly, you can stay on track with your business plan and make necessary adjustments to achieve your goals.

Establishing Accountability And Responsibility For Each Milestone

Assign Ownership: Assign a specific individual or team to be responsible for each milestone. This ensures that someone is accountable for its completion.

Clarify Expectations: Clearly communicate the expectations for each milestone, including the desired outcome, deadline, and any specific requirements or guidelines.

Set Clear Metrics: Define specific metrics or key performance indicators (KPIs) that will be used to measure the success of each milestone. This provides a clear benchmark for accountability.

Provide Resources: Ensure that the individual or team responsible for a milestone has access to the necessary resources, including funding, personnel, and equipment, to achieve it.

Establish Reporting Procedures: Define how progress will be reported and tracked for each milestone. This could include regular check-ins, progress reports, or meetings.

Encourage Collaboration: Foster a culture of collaboration and teamwork to ensure that everyone is working together towards the common goal of achieving the milestones.

Celebrate Success: Acknowledge and celebrate the achievement of milestones to recognize the hard work and effort put in by the team.

Address Issues Promptly: If a milestone is at risk of not being achieved, address the issue promptly. Identify the root cause of the problem and take corrective action to get back on track.

By establishing clear accountability and responsibility for each milestone, you can ensure that progress is monitored effectively and that the business plan stays on track towards achieving its goals.

* * *

CHAPTER 12: MONITORING AND EVALUATION

Setting Up Systems For Regular Performance Monitoring

Setting up systems for regular performance monitoring is essential for ensuring that your business plan stays on track and that you can make informed decisions based on progress. Here's how you can do it:

Define Key Performance Indicators (KPIs): Identify the key metrics that align with your business goals and objectives. These could include financial metrics, customer metrics, operational metrics, etc.

Establish Baselines: Determine the starting point for each KPI to create a baseline for comparison. This will help you measure progress over time.

Set Targets: Define specific, measurable targets for each KPI. These targets should be realistic and achievable based on your business objectives.

Implement Monitoring Tools: Use tools and systems to track and monitor your KPIs regularly. This could include software, dashboards, or spreadsheets.

Schedule Regular Reviews: Set up a regular schedule for reviewing performance against your KPIs. This could be monthly, quarterly, or annually, depending on your business needs.

Analyze and Interpret Data: Analyze the data collected from your performance monitoring to identify trends, patterns, and areas for improvement.

Take Action: Use the insights gained from your performance monitoring to take corrective action or make strategic decisions to improve performance.

Communicate Results: Share the results of your performance monitoring with key stakeholders, such as employees, investors, or partners, to keep them informed and engaged.

Review and Improve: Regularly review your performance monitoring systems and processes to identify ways to improve their effectiveness.

By setting up systems for regular performance monitoring, you can ensure that your business plan remains relevant and that you can make data-driven decisions to drive success.

Establishing Key Performance Indicators (KPIs) For Success

Identify Your Goals: Start by clearly defining your business goals and objectives. These will serve as the foundation for determining your KPIs.

Align KPIs with Goals: Ensure that each KPI directly relates to a specific business goal or objective. This will help you focus on what matters most to your business's success.

Make KPIs SMART: Ensure that each KPI is Specific, Measurable, Achievable, Relevant, and Time-bound. This will make it easier to track and evaluate performance.

Choose Relevant Metrics: Select metrics that are relevant to your business and reflect progress towards your goals. For example, if your goal is to increase sales, relevant KPIs could include revenue growth, conversion rates, or customer acquisition costs.

Set Targets: Establish realistic targets for each KPI based on historical data, industry benchmarks, and your business objectives. Targets should be challenging yet achievable.

Track Consistently: Implement systems and processes to track your KPIs consistently over time. This could involve using software, dashboards, or manual tracking methods.

Review and Adjust: Regularly review your KPIs to assess performance and identify areas for improvement. Be prepared to adjust your KPIs and targets as your business evolves.

Communicate KPIs: Ensure that your team is aware of the KPIs and targets and understands how their work contributes to achieving them. Encourage transparency and accountability.

Use KPIs to Drive Action: Use the insights gained from your KPIs to make informed decisions and take action to improve performance. KPIs should not just be numbers but should drive meaningful change in your business.

By establishing KPIs that are aligned with your goals, relevant to your business, and regularly tracked and reviewed, you can effectively measure the success of your business plan and make informed decisions to drive your business forward.

Creating A Process For Ongoing Evaluation And Adaptation

Set Regular Evaluation Intervals: Schedule regular intervals for evaluating your business plan. This could be quarterly, bi-annually, or annually, depending on your business's needs and the pace of change in your industry.

Review Key Performance Indicators (KPIs): Evaluate your KPIs to assess the progress of your business plan. Identify trends, patterns, and areas for improvement.

Gather Feedback: Solicit feedback from stakeholders, including customers, employees, and partners. Use this feedback to identify strengths and weaknesses in your business plan.

Benchmark Against Competitors: Compare your performance against competitors to identify areas where you can improve or differentiate yourself.

Assess Market Conditions: Monitor market conditions and trends that may impact your business. Stay informed about changes in customer preferences, technology, and regulations.

Identify Opportunities and Threats: Conduct a SWOT (Strengths, Weaknesses, Opportunities, Threats) analysis to identify opportunities for growth and potential threats to your business.

Adapt Your Plan: Based on your evaluation, make necessary adjustments to your business plan. This could include revising goals, updating strategies, or reallocating resources.

Communicate Changes: Ensure that your team is informed about any changes to the business plan and understands their role in implementing them.

Monitor Results: After making changes, continue to monitor the results to ensure that they are having the desired impact. Be prepared to make further adjustments if needed.

By creating a process for ongoing evaluation and adaptation, you can ensure that your business plan remains dynamic and responsive to changing circumstances, increasing your chances of long-term success.

CONCLUSION

In conclusion, "Business Plan Alchemy: Transforming Ideas Into Successful Ventures" serves as your trusted guide in the realm of entrepreneurial magic and strategic acumen. As we wrap up this transformative journey, it's evident that the alchemical process of crafting a business plan goes beyond mere documentation—it's an art form that breathes life into your ideas.

Through the pages of this ebook, we've explored the nuances of visionary entrepreneurship and the structured precision of business planning. The alchemy lies not only in the conversion of concepts into plans but in the strategic fusion of creativity, market insight, and operational excellence.

Armed with innovative approaches to idea refinement, market positioning, and financial foresight, you're now equipped to navigate the intricacies of the business landscape. This guide has empowered you to attract investors, mitigate risks, and lay a robust foundation for your venture's success.

As you embark on the journey to transform your business dreams into tangible realities, remember that the alchemical process is ongoing. Continuously refine, adapt, and evolve your business plan to meet the dynamic challenges of the market.

May your entrepreneurial endeavors be fueled by the alchemy of creativity and strategy, resulting in sustainable growth, competitive advantage, and the realization of your aspirations. "Business Plan Alchemy" is more than a book; it's a catalyst for turning your ideas into triumphant ventures. The alchemical journey doesn't end here; it's a perpetual cycle of innovation and success. May your business thrive and flourish on this path of transformative alchemy.

www.ingramcontent.com/pod-product-compliance
Lightning Source LLC
Chambersburg PA
CBHW060122120726
48003CB00009B/2744